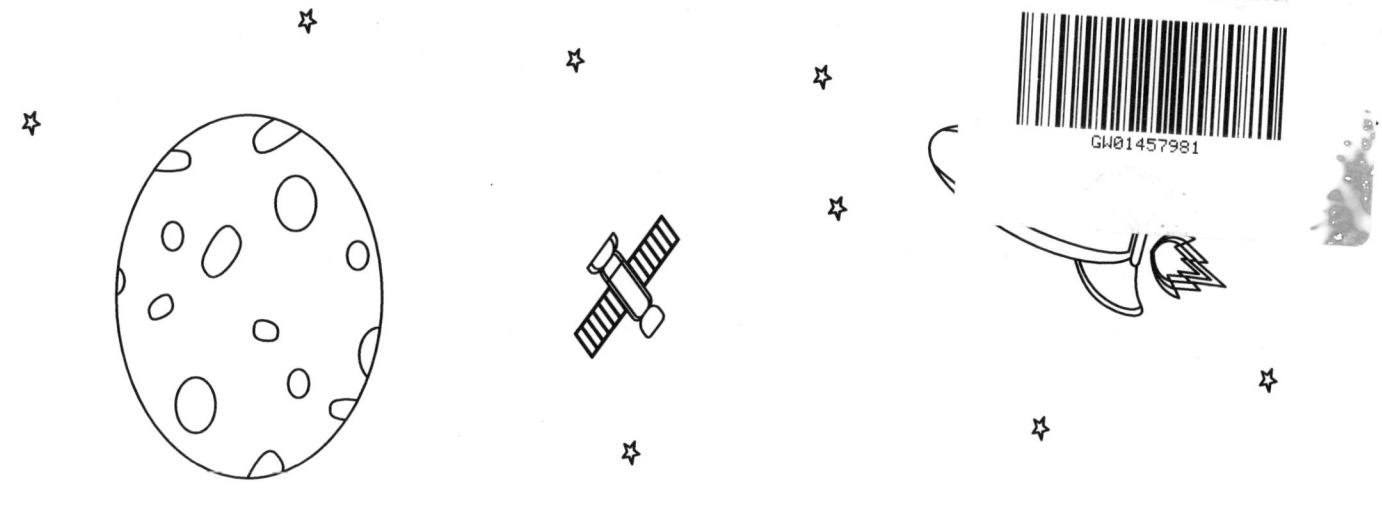

This book Belongs to:

★----------------------------★

★----------------------------★

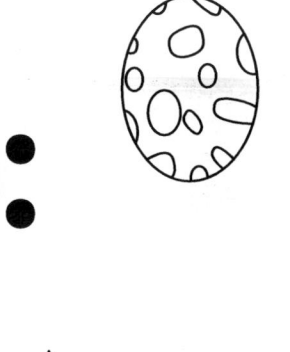

DATE: 1.1.23 TIME: 8 pm

LOCATION: ZIZI

What kind of object did you see?

- Moon ☑
- Planet ☑
- Galaxy ☑
- Star ☑
- Comet ☑
- Constellation ☑

Drawing object:

Moon phase:

Rating adventure:

My Notes:

DATE: _____ ⭑   TIME: _____ ⭑

LOCATION: _____ ⭑

What kind of object did you see?

- Moon ☐
- Planet ☐
- Galaxy ☐
- Star ☐
- Comet ☐
- Constellation ☐

Drawing object:

Moon phase:

Rating adventure:

Ok   Good   Really good   Fantastic   Amazing

My Notes:

★ - ★
★ - ★
★ - ★
★ - ★
★ - ★
★ - ★

DATE: _____ TIME: _____

LOCATION: _____

What kind of object did you see?

- Moon ☐
- Star ☐
- Planet ☐
- Comet ☐
- Galaxy ☐
- Constellation ☐

Drawing object:

Moon phase:

Rating adventure:

My Notes:

DATE: _____ ★   TIME: _____ ★

LOCATION: _____ ★

What kind of object did you see?

- Moon ☐
- Planet ☐
- Galaxy ☐
- Star ☐
- Comet ☐
- Constellation ☐

Drawing object:

Moon phase:

Rating adventure:

My Notes:

DATE: _____ TIME: _____

LOCATION: _____

What kind of object did you see?

- Moon ☐
- Star ☐
- Planet ☐
- Comet ☐
- Galaxy ☐
- Constellation ☐

Drawing object:

Moon phase:

Rating adventure:

Ok   Good   Really good   Fantastic   Amazing

My Notes:

★ - ★
★ - ★
★ - ★
★ - ★
★ - ★
★ - ★

DATE: _____ ★   TIME: _____ ★

LOCATION: _____ ★

What kind of object did you see?

- Moon ☐
- Planet ☐
- Galaxy ☐
- Star ☐
- Comet ☐
- Constellation ☐

Drawing object:

Moon phase:

Rating adventure:

Ok | Good | Really good | Fantastic | Amazing

My Notes:

★ - ★
★ - ★
★ - ★
★ - ★
★ - ★
★ - ★

DATE: _____ ★   TIME: _____ ★

LOCATION: _____ ★

What kind of object did you see?

- 🌙 Moon ☐
- 🪐 Planet ☐
- 🌌 Galaxy ☐
- ☆ Star ☐
- ☄ Comet ☐
- ✦ Constellation ☐

Drawing object:

Moon phase:

Rating adventure:

Ok Good Really good Fantastic Amazing

My Notes:

★ - ★
★ - ★
★ - ★
★ - ★
★ - ★
★ - ★

DATE: _____ TIME: _____

LOCATION: _____

What kind of object did you see?

- Moon ☐
- Planet ☐
- Galaxy ☐
- Star ☐
- Comet ☐
- Constellation ☐

Drawing object:

Moon phase:

Rating adventure:

Ok   Good   Really good   Fantastic   Amazing

My Notes:

★------------------------------★
★------------------------------★
★------------------------------★
★------------------------------★
★------------------------------★
★------------------------------★

DATE: _____ ★   TIME: _____ ★

LOCATION: _____ ★

What kind of object did you see?

- Moon ☐
- Star ☐
- Planet ☐
- Comet ☐
- Galaxy ☐
- Constellation ☐

Drawing object:

Moon phase:

Rating adventure:

Ok   Good   Really good   Fantastic   Amazing

My Notes:

★--★
★--★
★--★
★--★
★--★
★--★

DATE: _____ ★ TIME: _____ ★

LOCATION: _____ ★

What kind of object did you see?

- Moon ☐
- Star ☐
- Planet ☐
- Comet ☐
- Galaxy ☐
- Constellation ☐

Drawing object:

Moon phase:

Rating adventure:

My Notes:

★ - ★
★ - ★
★ - ★
★ - ★
★ - ★
★ - ★

DATE: _____ TIME: _____

LOCATION: _____

What kind of object did you see?

- Moon ☐
- Planet ☐
- Galaxy ☐
- Star ☐
- Comet ☐
- Constellation ☐

Drawing object:

Moon phase:

Rating adventure:

Ok Good Really good Fantastic Amazing

My Notes:

★ - ★
★ - ★
★ - ★
★ - ★
★ - ★
★ - ★

DATE: _____ TIME: _____

LOCATION: _____

What kind of object did you see?

- Moon ☐
- Star ☐
- Planet ☐
- Comet ☐
- Galaxy ☐
- Constellation ☐

Drawing object:

Moon phase:

Rating adventure:

Ok   Good   Really good   Fantastic   Amazing

My Notes:

★---------------------------------------★
★---------------------------------------★
★---------------------------------------★
★---------------------------------------★
★---------------------------------------★
★---------------------------------------★

DATE: _____ ★ TIME: _____ ★

LOCATION: _____ ★

What kind of object did you see?

- Moon ☐
- Planet ☐
- Galaxy ☐
- Star ☐
- Comet ☐
- Constellation ☐

Drawing object:

Moon phase:

Rating adventure:

Ok   Good   Really good   Fantastic   Amazing

My Notes:

★---★
★---★
★---★
★---★
★---★
★---★

DATE: _____ TIME: _____

LOCATION: _____

What kind of object did you see?

- 🌙 Moon ☐
- ⭐ Star ☐
- 🪐 Planet ☐
- ☄ Comet ☐
- 🌀 Galaxy ☐
- ✦ Constellation ☐

Drawing object:

Moon phase:

Rating adventure:

Ok   Good   Really good   Fantastic   Amazing

My Notes:

★ - ★
★ - ★
★ - ★
★ - ★
★ - ★
★ - ★

DATE: _____ TIME: _____

LOCATION: _____

What kind of object did you see?

- Moon ☐
- Star ☐
- Planet ☐
- Comet ☐
- Galaxy ☐
- Constellation ☐

Drawing object:

Moon phase:

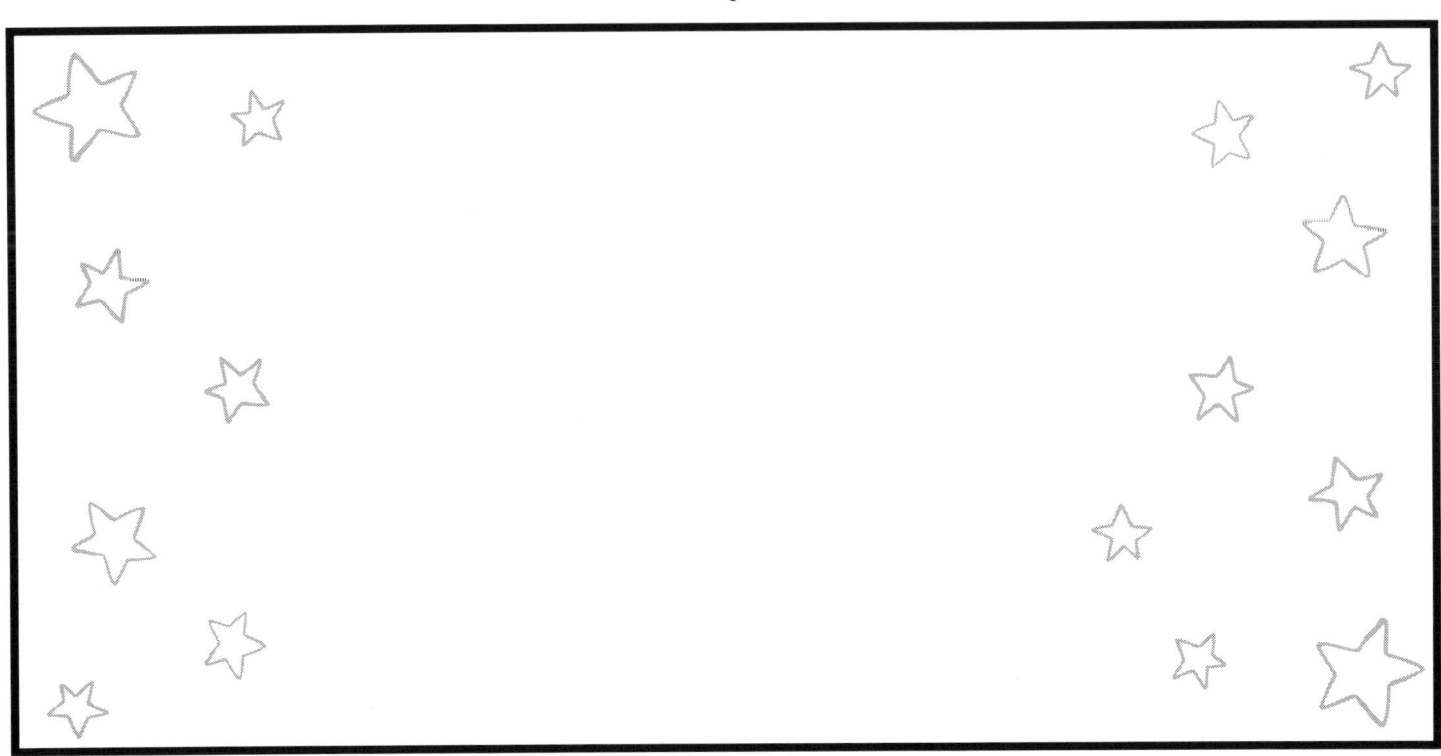

Rating adventure:

Ok   Good   Really good   Fantastic   Amazing

My Notes:

★ -- ★
★ -- ★
★ -- ★
★ -- ★
★ -- ★
★ -- ★

DATE: ＿＿＿＿＿＿＿＿＿ TIME: ＿＿＿＿＿＿＿＿＿

LOCATION: ＿＿＿＿＿＿＿＿＿

What kind of object did you see?

- Moon ☐
- Planet ☐
- Galaxy ☐
- Star ☐
- Comet ☐
- Constellation ☐

Drawing object:

Moon phase:

Rating adventure:

My Notes:

★------------------------------★
★------------------------------★
★------------------------------★
★------------------------------★
★------------------------------★
★------------------------------★

DATE: ⋯⋯⋯⋯⋯★ TIME: ⋯⋯⋯⋯⋯★

LOCATION: ⋯⋯⋯⋯⋯★

What kind of object did you see?

- 🌙 Moon ☐
- ⭐ Star ☐
- 🪐 Planet ☐
- ☄ Comet ☐
- 🌌 Galaxy ☐
- Constellation ☐

Drawing object:

Moon phase:

Rating adventure:

Ok   Good   Really good   Fantastic   Amazing

My Notes:

★ - ★
★ - ★
★ - ★
★ - ★
★ - ★
★ - ★

DATE: _____ TIME: _____

LOCATION: _____

What kind of object did you see?

- Moon ☐
- Star ☐
- Planet ☐
- Comet ☐
- Galaxy ☐
- Constellation ☐

Drawing object:

Moon phase:

Rating adventure:

Ok Good Really good Fantastic Amazing

My Notes:

★------------------------------------★
★------------------------------------★
★------------------------------------★
★------------------------------------★
★------------------------------------★
★------------------------------------★

DATE: _____ ★   TIME: _____ ★

LOCATION: _____ ★

What kind of object did you see?

- Moon ☐
- Planet ☐
- Galaxy ☐
- Star ☐
- Comet ☐
- Constellation ☐

Drawing object:

Moon phase:

Rating adventure:

Ok   Good   Really good   Fantastic   Amazing

My Notes:

★ -- ★
★ -- ★
★ -- ★
★ -- ★
★ -- ★
★ -- ★

DATE: _____ TIME: _____

LOCATION: _____

What kind of object did you see?

- Moon ☐
- Star ☐
- Planet ☐
- Comet ☐
- Galaxy ☐
- Constellation ☐

Drawing object:

Moon phase:

Rating adventure:

Ok   Good   Really good   Fantastic   Amazing

My Notes:

★---★
★---★
★---★
★---★
★---★
★---★

DATE: _____ TIME: _____

LOCATION: _____

What kind of object did you see?

- Moon ☐
- Planet ☐
- Galaxy ☐
- Star ☐
- Comet ☐
- Constellation ☐

Drawing object:

Moon phase:

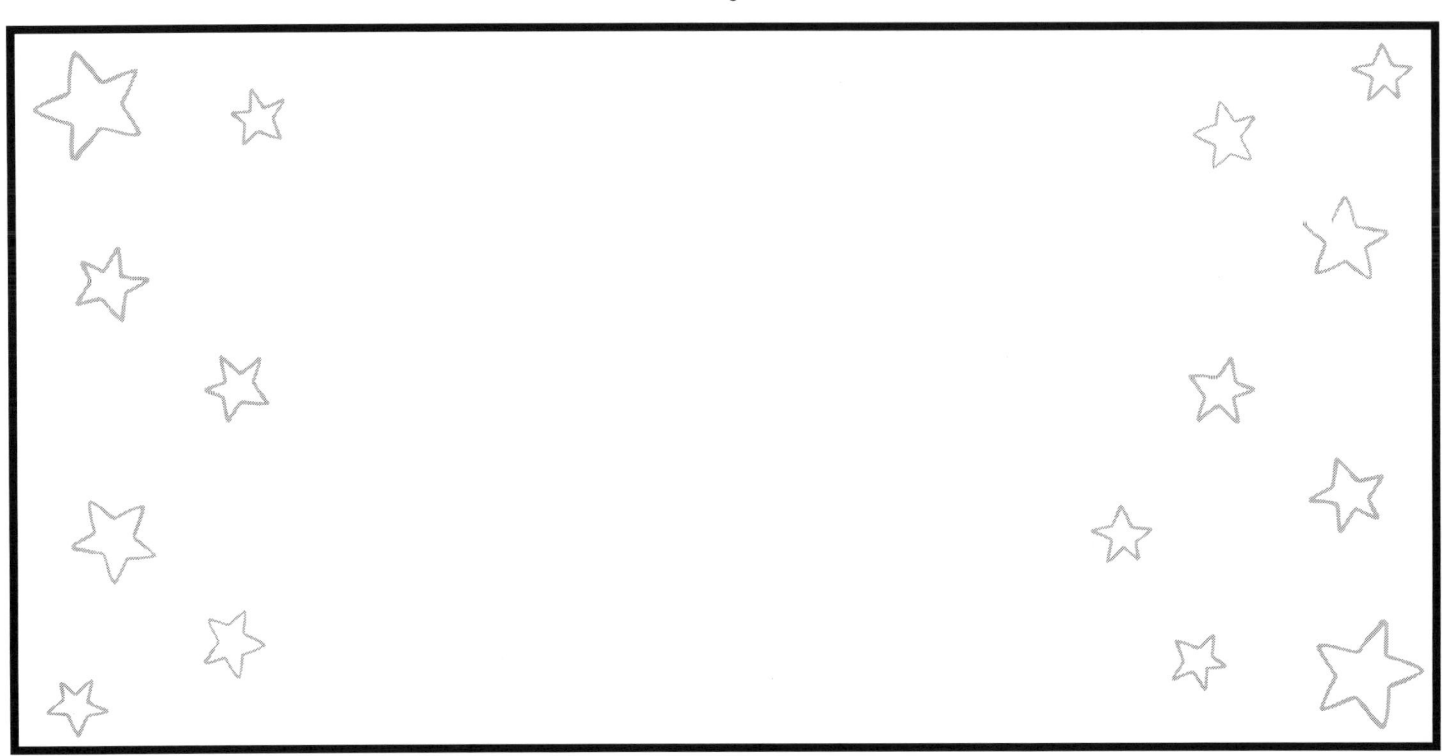

Rating adventure:

Ok   Good   Really good   Fantastic   Amazing

My Notes:

★ - ★
★ - ★
★ - ★
★ - ★
★ - ★
★ - ★

DATE: _____ TIME: _____

LOCATION: _____

What kind of object did you see?

- Moon ☐
- Star ☐
- Planet ☐
- Comet ☐
- Galaxy ☐
- Constellation ☐

Drawing object:

Moon phase:

Rating adventure:

Ok   Good   Really good   Fantastic   Amazing

My Notes:

★ - ★
★ - ★
★ - ★
★ - ★
★ - ★
★ - ★

DATE: _____ ★   TIME: _____ ★

LOCATION: _____ ★

What kind of object did you see?

- Moon ☐
- Star ☐
- Planet ☐
- Comet ☐
- Galaxy ☐
- Constellation ☐

Drawing object:

Moon phase:

Rating adventure:

Ok Good Really good Fantastic Amazing

My Notes:

★--★
★--★
★--★
★--★
★--★
★--★

DATE: _____ TIME: _____

LOCATION: _____

What kind of object did you see?

- Moon ☐
- Planet ☐
- Galaxy ☐
- Star ☐
- Comet ☐
- Constellation ☐

Drawing object:

Moon phase:

Rating adventure:

Ok　　Good　　Really good　　Fantastic　　Amazing

My Notes:

★--★
★--★
★--★
★--★
★--★
★--★

DATE: _____ TIME: _____

LOCATION: _____

What kind of object did you see?

- Moon ☐
- Star ☐
- Planet ☐
- Comet ☐
- Galaxy ☐
- Constellation ☐

Drawing object:

Moon phase:

Rating adventure:

Ok   Good   Really good   Fantastic   Amazing

My Notes:

★ - ★
★ - ★
★ - ★
★ - ★
★ - ★
★ - ★

DATE: _____ ✶   TIME: _____ ✶

LOCATION: _____ ✶

What kind of object did you see?

- Moon ☐
- Star ☐
- Planet ☐
- Comet ☐
- Galaxy ☐
- Constellation ☐

Drawing object:

Moon phase:

Rating adventure:

My Notes:

★ - ★
★ - ★
★ - ★
★ - ★
★ - ★
★ - ★

DATE: _____ TIME: _____

LOCATION: _____

What kind of object did you see?

- Moon ☐
- Star ☐
- Planet ☐
- Comet ☐
- Galaxy ☐
- Constellation ☐

Drawing object:

Moon phase:

Rating adventure:

Ok   Good   Really good   Fantastic   Amazing

My Notes:

★ - ★
★ - ★
★ - ★
★ - ★
★ - ★
★ - ★

DATE: _____ TIME: _____

LOCATION: _____

What kind of object did you see?

- Moon ☐
- Star ☐
- Planet ☐
- Comet ☐
- Galaxy ☐
- Constellation ☐

Drawing object:

Moon phase:

Rating adventure:

Ok Good Really good Fantastic Amazing

My Notes:

★---------------------------------★
★---------------------------------★
★---------------------------------★
★---------------------------------★
★---------------------------------★
★---------------------------------★

DATE: _____ TIME: _____

LOCATION: _____

What kind of object did you see?

- Moon ☐
- Planet ☐
- Galaxy ☐
- Star ☐
- Comet ☐
- Constellation ☐

Drawing object:

Moon phase:

Rating adventure:

My Notes:

DATE: _____ TIME: _____

LOCATION: _____

What kind of object did you see?

- Moon ☐
- Planet ☐
- Galaxy ☐
- Star ☐
- Comet ☐
- Constellation ☐

Drawing object:

Moon phase:

Rating adventure:

Ok Good Really good Fantastic Amazing

My Notes:

★ - ★
★ - ★
★ - ★
★ - ★
★ - ★
★ - ★

DATE: _____ ★   TIME: _____ ★

LOCATION: _____ ★

What kind of object did you see?

- Moon ☐
- Star ☐
- Planet ☐
- Comet ☐
- Galaxy ☐
- Constellation ☐

Drawing object:

Moon phase:

Rating adventure:

My Notes:

★ -- ★
★ -- ★
★ -- ★
★ -- ★
★ -- ★
★ -- ★

DATE: .... ★   TIME: .... ★

LOCATION: .... ★

What kind of object did you see?

- Moon ☐
- Star ☐
- Planet ☐
- Comet ☐
- Galaxy ☐
- Constellation ☐

Drawing object:

Moon phase:

Rating adventure:

| Ok | Good | Really good | Fantastic | Amazing |

My Notes:

★ ---------------------------------- ★
★ ---------------------------------- ★
★ ---------------------------------- ★
★ ---------------------------------- ★
★ ---------------------------------- ★
★ ---------------------------------- ★

DATE: _____ TIME: _____

LOCATION: _____

What kind of object did you see?

- Moon ☐
- Planet ☐
- Galaxy ☐
- Star ☐
- Comet ☐
- Constellation ☐

Drawing object:

Moon phase:

Rating adventure:

My Notes:

★ -- ★
★ -- ★
★ -- ★
★ -- ★
★ -- ★
★ -- ★

DATE: .... ★   TIME: .... ★

LOCATION: .... ★

What kind of object did you see?

- Moon ☐
- Star ☐
- Planet ☐
- Comet ☐
- Galaxy ☐
- Constellation ☐

Drawing object:

Moon phase:

Rating adventure:

My Notes:

★ - ★
★ - ★
★ - ★
★ - ★
★ - ★
★ - ★

DATE: _____ TIME: _____

LOCATION: _____

What kind of object did you see?

- Moon ☐
- Star ☐
- Planet ☐
- Comet ☐
- Galaxy ☐
- Constellation ☐

Drawing object:

Moon phase:

Rating adventure:

Ok   Good   Really good   Fantastic   Amazing

My Notes:

★ ------------------------------ ★
★ ------------------------------ ★
★ ------------------------------ ★
★ ------------------------------ ★
★ ------------------------------ ★
★ ------------------------------ ★

DATE: _____ ★   TIME: _____ ★

LOCATION: _____ ★

What kind of object did you see?

- 🌙 Moon ☐
- ⭐ Star ☐
- 🪐 Planet ☐
- ☄️ Comet ☐
- 🌀 Galaxy ☐
- ✧ Constellation ☐

Drawing object:

Moon phase:

Rating adventure:

Ok   Good   Really good   Fantastic   Amazing

My Notes:

★ -- ★
★ -- ★
★ -- ★
★ -- ★
★ -- ★
★ -- ★

DATE: _____ TIME: _____

LOCATION: _____

What kind of object did you see?

- Moon ☐
- Star ☐
- Planet ☐
- Comet ☐
- Galaxy ☐
- Constellation ☐

Drawing object:

Moon phase:

Rating adventure:

My Notes:

★ -- ★
★ -- ★
★ -- ★
★ -- ★
★ -- ★
★ -- ★

DATE: _____ TIME: _____

LOCATION: _____

What kind of object did you see?

- Moon ☐
- Star ☐
- Planet ☐
- Comet ☐
- Galaxy ☐
- Constellation ☐

Drawing object:

Moon phase:

Rating adventure:

My Notes:

DATE: _____ ★ TIME: _____ ★

LOCATION: _____ ★

What kind of object did you see?

- Moon ☐
- Planet ☐
- Galaxy ☐
- Star ☐
- Comet ☐
- Constellation ☐

Drawing object:

Moon phase:

Rating adventure:

My Notes:

★--★
★--★
★--★
★--★
★--★
★--★

DATE: _____ TIME: _____

LOCATION: _____

What kind of object did you see?

- Moon ☐
- Planet ☐
- Galaxy ☐
- Star ☐
- Comet ☐
- Constellation ☐

Drawing object:

Moon phase:

Rating adventure:

My Notes:

★ - ★
★ - ★
★ - ★
★ - ★
★ - ★
★ - ★

DATE: _____ ★   TIME: _____ ★

LOCATION: _____ ★

What kind of object did you see?

- Moon ☐
- Planet ☐
- Galaxy ☐
- Star ☐
- Comet ☐
- Constellation ☐

Drawing object:

Moon phase:

Rating adventure:

My Notes:

★ - ★
★ - ★
★ - ★
★ - ★
★ - ★
★ - ★

DATE: _____ ★   TIME: _____ ★

LOCATION: _____ ★

What kind of object did you see?

- Moon ☐
- Star ☐
- Planet ☐
- Comet ☐
- Galaxy ☐
- Constellation ☐

Drawing object:

Moon phase:

Rating adventure:

My Notes:

DATE: _____ TIME: _____

LOCATION: _____

What kind of object did you see?

- Moon ☐
- Star ☐
- Planet ☐
- Comet ☐
- Galaxy ☐
- Constellation ☐

Drawing object:

Moon phase:

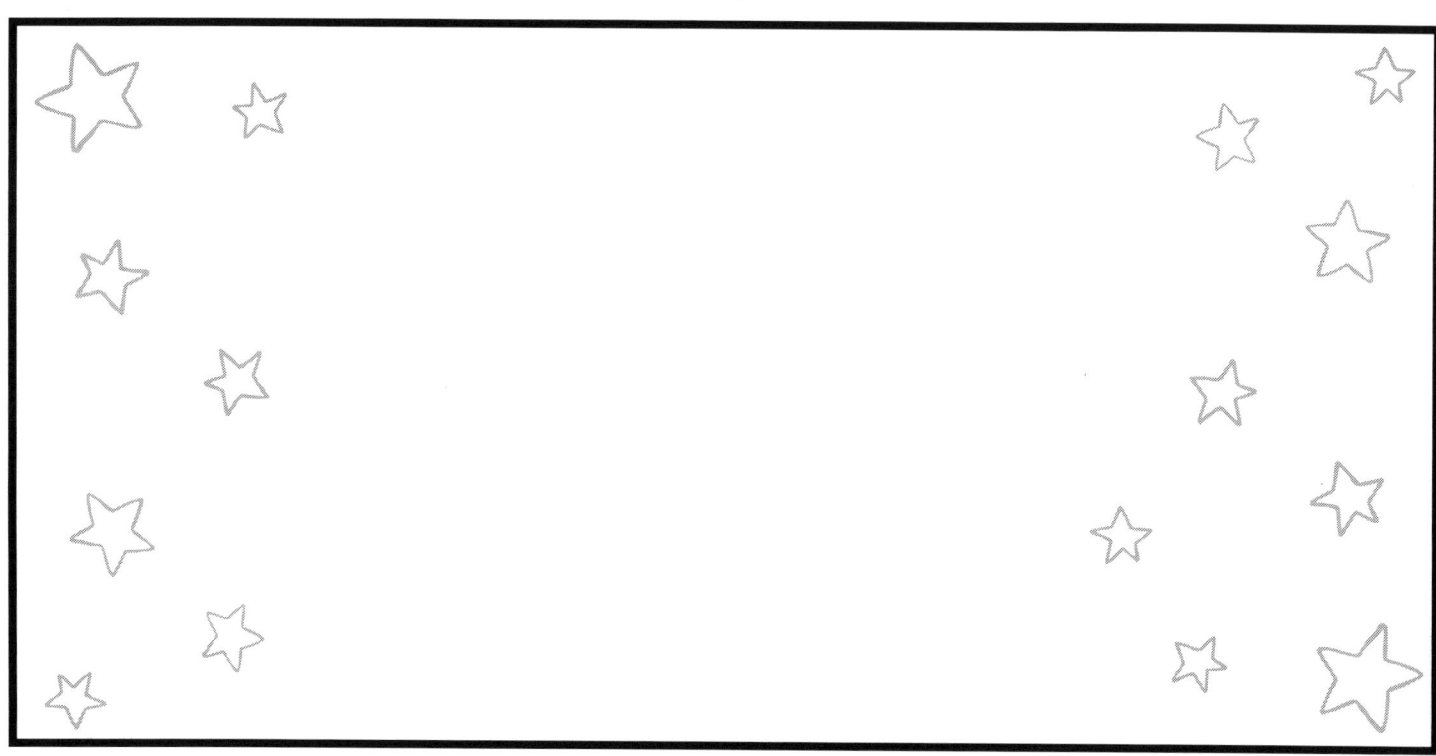

Rating adventure:

Ok Good Really good Fantastic Amazing

My Notes:

★------------------------------★
★------------------------------★
★------------------------------★
★------------------------------★
★------------------------------★
★------------------------------★

DATE: _____ ★   TIME: _____ ★

LOCATION: _____ ★

What kind of object did you see?

- Moon ☐
- Planet ☐
- Galaxy ☐
- Star ☐
- Comet ☐
- Constellation ☐

Drawing object:

Moon phase:

Rating adventure:

My Notes:

★ -- ★
★ -- ★
★ -- ★
★ -- ★
★ -- ★
★ -- ★

DATE: _____ ⭐   TIME: _____ ⭐

LOCATION: _____ ⭐

What kind of object did you see?

- Moon ☐
- Planet ☐
- Galaxy ☐
- Star ☐
- Comet ☐
- Constellation ☐

Drawing object:

Moon phase:

Rating adventure:

My Notes:

★ -- ★
★ -- ★
★ -- ★
★ -- ★
★ -- ★
★ -- ★

DATE: ……………………★   TIME: ……………………★

LOCATION: ……………………★

What kind of object did you see?

- Moon ☐
- Star ☐
- Planet ☐
- Comet ☐
- Galaxy ☐
- Constellation ☐

Drawing object:

Moon phase:

Rating adventure:

My Notes:

★ -- ★
★ -- ★
★ -- ★
★ -- ★
★ -- ★
★ -- ★

DATE: _____ ★   TIME: _____ ★

LOCATION: _____ ★

What kind of object did you see?

- Moon ☐
- Star ☐
- Planet ☐
- Comet ☐
- Galaxy ☐
- Constellation ☐

Drawing object:

Moon phase:

Rating adventure:

My Notes:

DATE: _____ TIME: _____

LOCATION: _____

What kind of object did you see?

- Moon ☐
- Planet ☐
- Galaxy ☐
- Star ☐
- Comet ☐
- Constellation ☐

Drawing object:

Moon phase:

Rating adventure:

My Notes:

DATE: _____ ★   TIME: _____ ★

LOCATION: _____ ★

What kind of object did you see?

- Moon ☐
- Star ☐
- Planet ☐
- Comet ☐
- Galaxy ☐
- Constellation ☐

Drawing object:

Moon phase:

Rating adventure:

Ok | Good | Really good | Fantastic | Amazing

My Notes:

★ -- ★
★ -- ★
★ -- ★
★ -- ★
★ -- ★
★ -- ★

DATE: ⋯⋯⋯⋯⋯★   TIME: ⋯⋯⋯⋯⋯★

LOCATION: ⋯⋯⋯⋯⋯★

What kind of object did you see?

- Moon ☐
- Star ☐
- Planet ☐
- Comet ☐
- Galaxy ☐
- Constellation ☐

Drawing object:

Moon phase:

Rating adventure:

My Notes:

★ --- ★
★ --- ★
★ --- ★
★ --- ★
★ --- ★
★ --- ★

DATE:_____ TIME:_____

LOCATION:_____

What kind of object did you see?

- Moon ☐
- Planet ☐
- Galaxy ☐
- Star ☐
- Comet ☐
- Constellation ☐

Drawing object:

Moon phase:

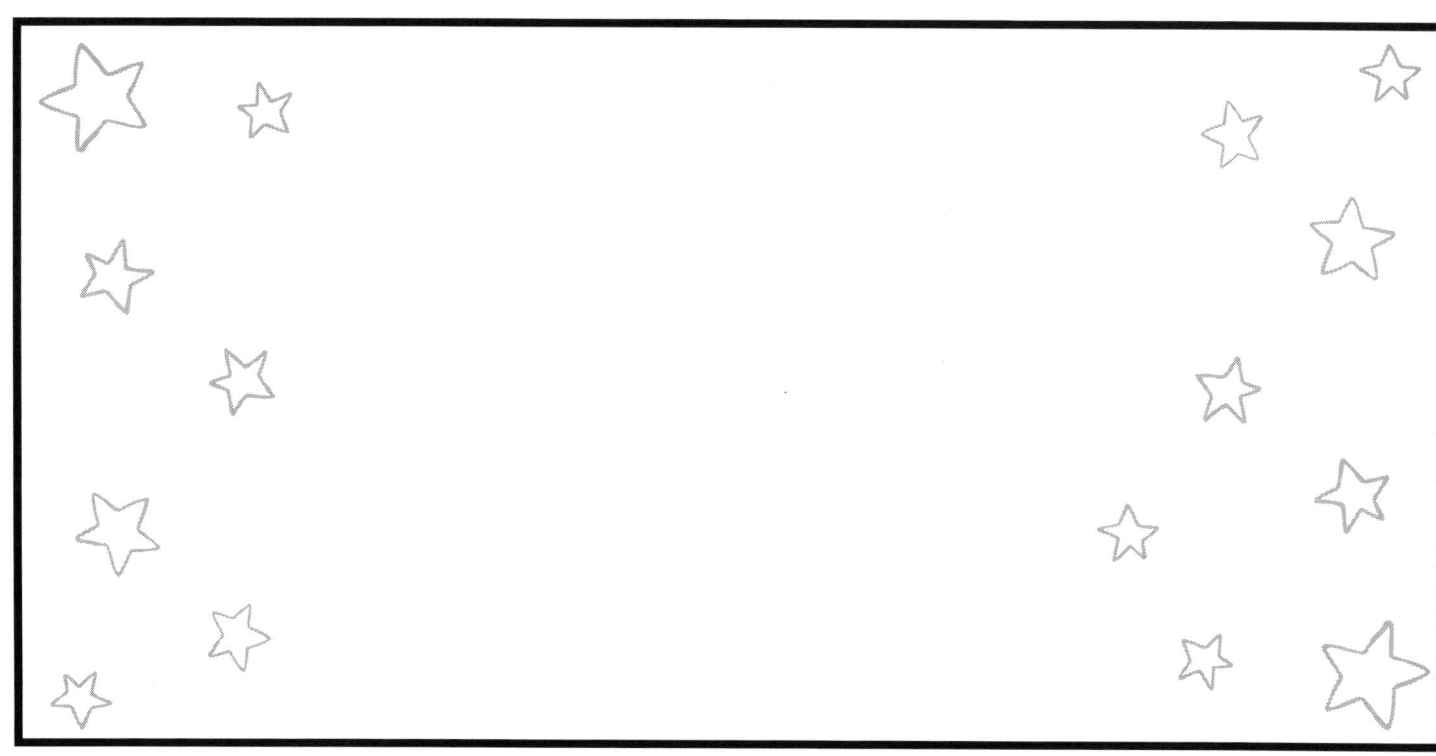

Rating adventure:

Ok   Good   Really good   Fantastic   Amazing

My Notes:

★ -- ★
★ -- ★
★ -- ★
★ -- ★
★ -- ★
★ -- ★

DATE: _____ ✱   TIME: _____ ✱

LOCATION: _____ ✱

What kind of object did you see?

- Moon ☐
- Star ☐
- Planet ☐
- Comet ☐
- Galaxy ☐
- Constellation ☐

Drawing object:

Moon phase:

Rating adventure:

My Notes:

DATE: .... ★   TIME: .... ★

LOCATION: .... ★

What kind of object did you see?

- Moon ☐
- Planet ☐
- Galaxy ☐
- Star ☐
- Comet ☐
- Constellation ☐

Drawing object:

Moon phase:

Rating adventure:

Ok | Good | Really good | Fantastic | Amazing

My Notes:

★ -- ★
★ -- ★
★ -- ★
★ -- ★
★ -- ★
★ -- ★

DATE: _____ TIME: _____

LOCATION: _____

What kind of object did you see?

- Moon ☐
- Star ☐
- Planet ☐
- Comet ☐
- Galaxy ☐
- Constellation ☐

Drawing object:

Moon phase:

Rating adventure:

My Notes:

★--★
★--★
★--★
★--★
★--★
★--★

DATE: .... ★   TIME: .... ★

LOCATION: .... ★

What kind of object did you see?

- Moon ☐
- Star ☐
- Planet ☐
- Comet ☐
- Galaxy ☐
- Constellation ☐

Drawing object:

Moon phase:

Rating adventure:

Ok   Good   Really good   Fantastic   Amazing

My Notes:

★ -- ★
★ -- ★
★ -- ★
★ -- ★
★ -- ★
★ -- ★

DATE: _____ TIME: _____

LOCATION: _____

What kind of object did you see?

- Moon ☐
- Star ☐
- Planet ☐
- Comet ☐
- Galaxy ☐
- Constellation ☐

Drawing object:

Moon phase:

Rating adventure:

My Notes:

★ --- ★
★ --- ★
★ --- ★
★ --- ★
★ --- ★
★ --- ★

DATE: _____ ★ TIME: _____ ★

LOCATION: _____ ★

What kind of object did you see?

- Moon ☐
- Star ☐
- Planet ☐
- Comet ☐
- Galaxy ☐
- Constellation ☐

Drawing object:

Moon phase:

Rating adventure:

My Notes:

★ - ★
★ - ★
★ - ★
★ - ★
★ - ★
★ - ★

DATE: _____ ★   TIME: _____ ★

LOCATION: _____ ★

What kind of object did you see?

- Moon ☐
- Star ☐
- Planet ☐
- Comet ☐
- Galaxy ☐
- Constellation ☐

Drawing object:

Moon phase:

Rating adventure:

My Notes:

★ -- ★
★ -- ★
★ -- ★
★ -- ★
★ -- ★
★ -- ★

DATE: _____ ⭑   TIME: _____ ⭑

LOCATION: _____ ⭑

What kind of object did you see?

🌙 Moon ☐   ☆ Star ☐

🪐 Planet ☐   ☄ Comet ☐

🌀 Galaxy ☐   ⋰ Constellation ☐

Drawing object:

Moon phase:

Rating adventure:

My Notes:

★ - ★
★ - ★
★ - ★
★ - ★
★ - ★
★ - ★

DATE: _____ TIME: _____

LOCATION: _____

What kind of object did you see?

- Moon ☐
- Planet ☐
- Galaxy ☐
- Star ☐
- Comet ☐
- Constellation ☐

Drawing object:

Printed in Great Britain
by Amazon